STRENGTH

A Daily Devotional For The Stay At
Home Mom

STRENGTH

A Daily Devotional For The Stay At
Home Mom

Jasmine Frost

Published by For His Glory Writing Co.
5792 Lakeshore Drive
Bean Station, TN 37708
www.forhisglorywc.com

Cover Photo by Diana Simumpande on Unsplash

Unless otherwise noted, all Scripture quotations are from the New King James Version of the Bible, Copyright © 1982 by Thomas Nelson.

ISBN: 9781790238637

Printed in the United States of America

FHG
FOR HIS GLORY

Contents

Introduction

An Open Letter to the Stay at Home Mom

My dear stay at home mommy,

You, like so many other women, wear multiple hats and your work is never done. We have all seen circus acts, when a clown juggles three to four balls simultaneously. Each one being tossed high in the air in a seemingly crazy manner. It seems impossible for the clown to catch them all. Low and behold, at the end of the act, the clown catches them all and with ease. This is a clear depiction of the life of a stay at home mom.

We juggle so many roles and responsibilities. In the midst of total chaos, we somehow manage to get it all done! It may look easy, but we know all too well that being a "mommager" can be one of the toughest jobs of all. Despite its many challenges and endless pursuits of keeping it all together; this unique role is especially rewarding. Seeing those precious little smiles when your children wake-up each morning makes it all worthwhile!

This devotional is filled with prayers, scriptures, and personal experiences that serve as a source of strength, support, and encouragement for the stay at home mommy. As you embark on your journey of being at home with the kiddos, know that God hears your prayers, sees the sweat and tears, and acknowledges your hard work and dedication to your family and home. Also, know that you are uniquely created for this role as a stay at home mom and "mommager". Take extra pride in knowing that God has entrusted you with this special purpose.

God bless you Woman of God!

Jasmine Frost

A Prayer

Lord, I pray that this daily devotional transforms mindsets, encourages, and instills a zeal and tenacity to continue to bear the cross you have given us as Christian women. I ask that your Holy Spirit reveal to each of my sisters in Christ, their divine purpose as a stay at home mom and the beauty that comes with this role. I pray that she embraces this responsibility with joy. Lastly, I pray that this mantle be used for your Glory to set an atmosphere of peace and love that will have a lasting impact on her husband, children, household, and ministry. In Jesus name I pray. Amen!

Defeating Negative Feelings

Combating Feelings of Inadequacy

As women, many times Satan plagues us with thoughts and feelings of inadequacy. When we entertain these thoughts, what began as a trickle, becomes a roaring flood of thoughts that consume our daily lives. Now that the floodgates are open, the comparison game dominates and devours our every existence. We begin comparing ourselves to other women and even our male counterparts.

As a stay at home mom, we begin thinking that we are a waste of space. That our job as a stay at home mom is deemed worthless. We begin thinking and even confessing openly that, "I am wasting my time; I could be doing something great, but I am at home with the children." Before you know it, we begin questioning God, "Is this my purpose?" "Is this all you have in store for me?" "Can I even handle being a stay at home mom?"

Feeling inadequate equates to feeling insufficient, incompetent, and discontent in your divine purpose. You must understand that as women we are to be "mommagers" of our homes. This is more than just being a manager; instead this a mandate and mantle! Meaning God has given you the authority to succeed in this extraordinary role. There is great honor that comes with managing your children and home in a way that is pleasing to the Lord. As we dive into scripture, meditate and confess these scriptures to combat the fiery darts of Satan and finally extinguish those negative feelings of inadequacy.

You Are A Role Model

In all things showing yourself to be a pattern of good works; in doctrine showing integrity, reverence, incorruptibility, sound speech that cannot be condemned, that one who is an opponent may be ashamed, having nothing evil to say of you.—**Titus 2:7-8**

Train up a child in the way he should go, And when he is old he will not depart from it.

—**Proverbs 22:6**

Wives, submit to your own husbands, as to the Lord. For the husband is head of the wife, as also Christ is head of the church; and He is the Savior of

The older women likewise, that they be reverent in behavior, not slanderers, not given to much wine, teachers of good things— that they admonish the young women to love their husbands, to love their children, to be discreet, chaste, homemakers, good, obedient to their own husbands, that the word of God may not be blasphemed.

Titus 2:3-5

the body. Therefore, just as the church is subject to Christ, so let the wives be to their own husbands in everything.

—Ephesians 5:22-24

PRAYER & CONFESSION

Dear Heavenly Father, we give thanks to you on this day and we lift my sister in Christ to you. We thank you, that you have graciously exposed the enemy as the opponent of these feelings of inadequacy. We know that Satan is the father of lies. We confess openly that we are good role models to others as women of God. As you have commanded we are equipped to train up our children in the admonition of our Lord and Savior Jesus Christ. We choose to serve the Lord with gladness and joy each day as we submit to our spouses, raise our children, and manage our homes.

We partner with the Holy Spirit and declare and decree that we walk with integrity, reverence, and incorruptibility. We also declare and decree that we love our spouses and children as Christ has deemed in the Holy Scriptures. As women of God we operate in discretion, we are chaste, we are homemakers, we speak with wisdom, we are good and obedient to the word of God. In Jesus name we pray. Amen.

You Have Help

I can do all things through Christ who strengthens me.

*—**Philippians** 4:13*

Let us therefore come boldly to the throne of grace, that we may obtain mercy and find grace to help in time of need.

*—**Hebrews 4:16***

*Fear not, for I am with you;
Be not dismayed,
for I am your God.
I will strengthen you,
Yes, I will help you,
I will uphold you with My righteous right hand.*

Isaiah 41:10

PRAYER & CONFESSION

Lord, we thank you that your grace and mercy renews with each morning. We thank you that you have graced us as stay at home moms to accomplish our daily tasks and with excellence. We ask for your divine and supernatural strength to overtake us and help us. We know that when we are weak, you make us strong. We know that your grace is sufficient enough and you are our ultimate source of strength.

No matter our current circumstance, we will trust you with our whole heart. We trust in your Holy word and on your promises because you are good, just, and provide for us daily. Lord Jesus, we want to take this moment to glorify your precious and Holy name because you will never leave nor forsake us. In our time of need, because of your never failing love, you will always be there for us. We confess openly with our mouths that the Lord is our help and strength. We give you thanks and shower you with honor on this day. In Jesus mighty name we pray. Amen.

You Are Secure

The Lord is my rock and my fortress and my deliverer;
My God, my strength, in whom I will trust;
My shield and the horn of my salvation, my stronghold

—Psalms 18:2

Have I not commanded you? Be strong and of good courage; do not be afraid, nor be dismayed, for the Lord your God is with you wherever you go.
—Joshua 1:9

Therefore, having been justified by faith, we have peace with God through our Lord Jesus Christ.—**Romans 5:1**

✝

PRAYER & CONFESSION

Dear God, we approach your throne of grace and mercy with humility. As stay at home moms we know that we are secure in our divine purpose. We are content with the responsibilities you have entrusted us with. We will serve you with gladness all the days our lives, and with every fiber of our being. With faith in the almighty, the alpha and omega, we acknowledge your agape love for us. Having this knowledge that your love for us is unconditional and incomprehensible, we overcome any feelings of insecurity.

We confess that we do not have a spirit of fear, but of power, love and a sound mind. You are our hope and our salvation. You are our rock and fortress, meaning you're our foundation that we can stand firm on, even through any negative feelings. We declare and decree that you are our stronghold. As your people, we are the sheep of your pasteur and you are the good shepherd. You lead us and guide us into all truth, and have chosen us to be a part of your Kingdom. We shall give you all of the honor, praise, and glory that we are made righteous through your faithfulness and therefore are secure forever. In Jesus name. Amen.

You Are Competent

The Lord is my light and my salvation ; Whom shall I fear? The Lord is the strength of my life; Of whom shall I be afraid?

—**Psalm 27:1**

Trust in the Lord with all your heart, And lean not on your own understanding; In all your ways acknowledge Him, And He shall direct your paths.

—**Proverbs 3:5-6**

And we have such trust through Christ toward God. Not that we are sufficient of ourselves to think of anything as being from ourselves, but our sufficiency is from God.

2 Corinthians 3:4-5

✝

PRAYER & CONFESSION

Heavenly Father, we thank you and rejoice because we know where our competence comes from. You have formed us in the womb, and have uniquely created us to be mothers. We will bear this responsibility with wisdom, understanding, and the authority to carry out the mantle. We will not lean on our own understanding of our current circumstance; however, we will acknowledge you Lord. We declare and decree that we see things through the eyes, heart, and mind of Christ. We now acknowledge that you will lead and direct our paths each day.

By the guidance of the Holy Spirit, we are made sufficient in our responsibilities as stay at home moms. We will succeed and be victorious in our roles as wives, mothers, and "mommagers" of our homes. Because of the blood of your precious and only son, Jesus Christ, we are deemed worthy. We are worthy of passing the baton of wisdom and knowledge to our sons and daughters as we raise them up in the admonition of the Lord. In Jesus name we pray. Amen.

~~Defeating Negative Feelings~~

Fighting Feelings of Frustration

More days than none, the screaming; the whining and crying; the clanging and banging of toys; the constant "mommy, mommy," can just about drive the strongest and most patient of women up the wall! The mountains of dirty clothes and dishes piling up so high you'd think we have never washed a piece of clothing or a dish in our entire lives. Each day, there are countless tasks on our to-do lists which seems endless.

Between cleaning, cooking, and caring for the children; getting a shower or some alone time in the bathroom becomes more and more of a luxury. Unlike regular employees, there are no allotted lunch breaks or paid time off. Many times we just want to throw in the towel, run and hide, and bawl our eyes out. The feelings of being overwhelmed mixed with irritation, failure, and even anger begins to suffocate us.

Does this sound like any of you? I know this struggle all too well! I know many of you may be wondering, "how do I actually overcome these feelings though?" The answer is quite simple, but yet oh so complicated. A change of our perspective is the key to unlocking the door of victory over these taunting feelings of frustration. A change of our perspective on the situation, will soften our hearts toward our children and this mantle and mandate of being a "mommager". Even when our children and current circumstances pushes us to our limits; a shift in our current mindset to the heart and mind of Christ is vital. When this occurs, all frustration, anger, and feelings of being overwhelmed have to flee! The burden and the load of our daily tasks as stay at home moms will begin to lighten with each passing day as our minds are being renewed.

Remember, the heart and mind of Christ is rooted in agape or unconditional love. According to 1 Peter 4:8, love covers a multitude of sin. In the midst of hardship: instances of when our children are being rebellious, disobedient, and just plain acting out; our pure, unconditional love for them, coupled with the joy of the Lord and a shift in our mindset allows us to successfully combat these negative feelings. As you read, confess, and meditate on the scriptures below allow this living water to flow into the river of your heart and give you a fresh perspective on your life. Your life and role as a stay at home mom is seen as precious in the sight of the almighty!

You Have Joy

Do not grieve, for the joy of the Lord is your strength.
—Nehemiah 8:10

Now may the God of hope fill you with all joy and peace in believing, that you may abound in hope by the power of the Holy Spirit.

Romans 15:13

My brethren, count it all joy when you fall into various trials, knowing that the testing of your faith produces patience.
—James 1:2-3

PRAYER & CONFESSION

Dear Heavenly Father we glorify you on this day, because you have given us a revelation on how to fight against these feelings of frustration that try to overtake us. We take captive every negative thought that exalts itself against your Holy word. We do not entertain these thoughts; however, we meditate on your word as the foundation that guides our thoughts, actions, and behavior. We now understand that our children are learning from us and model our behavior.

We acknowledge an understanding that when we become upset and frustrated, these feelings are sensed and transferred to our children. As we pray and confess your Holy scriptures, we thank you that our perspectives are changing right now. That we will not conform to the ways of this world, but will be transformed with the renewing of our minds daily. We approve your good and perfect will over our lives as stay at home moms according to Romans 12:2.

We thank you that this impartation of revelation knowledge is made alive in each of us in a meaningful way. Although we may have some adversity as stay at home moms, we count it all as joy because through these trials we are producing patience; a fruit of your spirit Lord. We declare and decree that we will pass every test from this day forth, and that our faith is increased to another level of glory. In Jesus name we pray. Amen.

You Have Love

The Lord will fulfill his purpose for me; your steadfast love, O LORD, endures forever.

—Psalm 138:8

And now abide faith, hope, love, these three; but the greatest of these is love.

—1 Corinthians 13:13

Love suffers long and is kind; love does not envy; love does not parade itself, is not puffed up; does not behave rudely, does not seek its own, is not provoked, thinks no evil; does not rejoice in iniquity, but rejoices in the truth; bears all things, believes all things, hopes all things, endures all things. Love never fails.

1 Corinthians 13:4-8

PRAYER & CONFESSION

Lord Jesus Christ, we approach your throne of grace and mercy as humbly as we know how. As we continue on our journey as stay at home moms, we will fulfill this purpose in love. Love for our husbands, love for our children, and love for the mandate and mantle of this unique responsibility. We now understand that love is the greatest gift of all. It was with love that you, Father God, gave your only begotten son to die for us. It was because of the love for his Father, that Jesus was willing and able to sacrifice his life for man.

We acknowledge that anything we pursue in this life, if it is done without the love of Christ, then we do it all in vain. We declare and decree that we will ever abide in hope, faith, and most importantly love. While we are carrying out this duty as stay at home moms, we will not be provoked to frustration, wrath, or evil thinking. We will instead, behave kindly and patiently. We will continue to bear all things, hope all things, and endure all things because love never fails. In Jesus mighty name we pray. Amen.

You Have Peace

And the peace of God, which surpasses all understanding, will guard your hearts and minds through Christ Jesus.

—**Philippians 4:7**

And let the peace of God rule in your hearts, to which also you were called in one body; and be thankful.

—**Colossians 3:15**

But the fruit of the Spirit is love, joy, peace, longsuffering, kindness, goodness, faithfulness, gentleness, self-control.

Galatians 5:22-23

✝

PRAYER & CONFESSION

Father God in Heaven, we want to give you praise on today because you have gifted us with the fruits of your Holy Spirit. We will not fulfill the lusts of the flesh, but walk by the spirit in love, joy, peace, patience, kindness, goodness, faithfulness, gentleness, and self-control. As we are being led by the spirit, all frustration, irritation, anger, and wrath have to flee.

Therefore, in Christ we have liberty according to Galatians chapter 5! We are free from all spirits of oppression and frustration. We are free from any and all bondages that are trying to yoke, choke, and hinder us from walking in the fullness of our calling as stay at home moms. As the revelation of the peace of God rules and abides in our hearts; we honor and glorify your precious and Holy name Father God. We ask you Lord, that we begin living a lifestyle of peace; this peace that surpasses all understanding. We declare and decree that your peace surrounds and guards our hearts and minds each day. In Jesus name we pray. Amen.

You Will Succeed

But thanks be to God, who gives us the victory through our Lord Jesus Christ.—**1 Corinthians 15:57**

Commit your works to the Lord, And your thoughts will be established.—**Proverbs 16:1**

But his delight is in the law of the Lord, And in His law he meditates day and night. He shall be like a tree Planted by the rivers of water, That brings forth its fruit in its season, Whose leaf also shall not wither; And whatever he does shall prosper.

Psalms 1:2-3

PRAYER & CONFESSION

Dear Heavenly Father, according to 1 Kings 2:3, as we walk in your required obedience; we will be prosperous and successful in every area of our lives as stay at home moms. As lovers and followers of Christ, we will continue to commit ourselves to the works of the Lord. As our commitment to you and our families deepen, our thoughts and our plans will be established. Our thoughts and plans of good and not evil for our family and household will ensue.

Lord, we will delight in you and your Holy word. As we delight in you, and meditate on your Holy word day and night; we will be made firm as a tree. Our thoughts and actions will be rooted in the living word. We thank you for your grace as we grow and mature in our walk as followers of Christ and stay at home moms. We declare and decree that we will bear good fruit that will never rot and wither. This good fruit is the outward expression of our household prospering! We thank you that our thoughts, actions, and behaviors are being transformed into the likeness of Christ as our souls prosper an abundant harvest. In Jesus name we pray, Amen.

~~Defeating Negative Feelings~~

Leveling Feelings of Loneliness

The glitz and glam of becoming a mother, oftentimes overshadows the fact that we need encouragement, support, and meaningful relationships. As stay at home moms, we become so consumed with attending to the needs of our families, that we forget to attend to our own wellness. Then we begin to realize, we have no life outside of the children. Meaningful relationships with other adults become a faint glimmer of your old existence.

As a result, feelings of loneliness begin to manifest and linger. This loneliness starts subtly, until the hole is so deep that it appears black and bottomless. As we stand at the edge of this black, empty hole; Satan tries to push us head first into this bottomless pit of loneliness and depression. Satan takes pleasure at seeing us residing in this place of utter torment.

As followers of Christ, we are not of this world; however, this does not mean you lock yourself away from building healthy relationships with others—especially among the Kingdom. Satan's tactics are to divide and conquer. Once division strikes, a house cannot stand according to Mark 3:24-26. Do not allow Satan to push you over the edge into a black, bottomless pit where all hope is lost and you are divided from God's people. Choose to rest and reside in the presence of the Holy One and amongst a Kingdom network of believers who can pour into you spiritually, mentally, and physically. As a stay at home mom, your overall wellness is critical to the overall wellness and optimal function of your household!

You Are Not Alone

...For He Himself has said, "I will never leave you nor forsake you."—**Hebrews 13:5**

And the Lord, He is the One who goes before you. He will be with you, He will not leave you nor forsake you; do not fear nor be dismayed."—**Deuteronomy 31:8**

But You, O Lord,
are a shield for
me,
My glory and the
One who lifts up
my head.
I cried to the
Lord with my
voice,
And He heard me
from His holy
hill.

Psalms 3:3-4

†

PRAYER & CONFESSION

Dear Heavenly Father, we love you and fully trust that you will never leave nor forsake us as your Holy Scriptures says. We are so thankful that when we feel like we are in a lonely pit, you hear our cries and will pull us out of this desolate place. You will quickly remind us that we are truly never alone. Your Holy Spirit is among us and closer than we think.

According to Psalms 40:2, you have lifted us out of this horrible pit of loneliness and depression. You have lifted us out of the miry clay, and have now set our feet upon a rock. Lord, we give you the honor, glory, and praise you deserve because we are blessed and highly favored. We declare and decree we are the head and not the tail; we are above and not beneath according to Deuteronomy 28:13. Jesus, thank you for the compassion you have for your people; you understand our struggles and still love us despite our faults. When we cry, you cry and intercede in prayer for us to the Father. We give you honor because you are a good and just God. In Jesus name we pray. Amen.

You Have Encouragement

Cast all your anxiety on him because he cares for you.

—1 Peter 5:7

For I know the thoughts that I think toward you, says the Lord, thoughts of peace and not of evil, to give you a future and a hope.

—Jeremiah 29:11

Blessed be the God and Father of our Lord Jesus Christ, the Father of mercies and God of all comfort, who comforts us in all our tribulation, that we may be able to comfort those who are in any trouble, with the comfort with which we ourselves are comforted by God.

2 Corinthians 1:3-4

PRAYER & CONFESSION

Dear Father God, we exalt your precious name. We are honored and humbled because you have a unique plan for each of us. We thank you because you have devised a plan for our future that will manifest nothing but blessings in due time. Although, we may be experiencing a season of loneliness in our pursuits as stay at home moms; we acknowledge your love, support, and encouragement. As we seek your face, we pray that your Holy Spirit blankets us with comfort in our time of need.

Heavenly Father, we call forth divine Kingdom connections with other adults. Lord, we give you thanks because you are sending the right people in our path who will pour into us wholeheartedly. We acknowledge that you are building healthy relational connections right now. These genuine connections will lead to a lifetime of fellowship and friendship. Again, we give you honor and praise, that these things are done in your perfect timing. In Jesus mighty name. Amen.

Defeating Negative Feelings

Warring Against Feelings of Weakness

Wearing multiple hats as a stay at home mom can be immensely tiring. Countless early mornings and late nights can wear on us physically, mentally, as well as spiritually. Many mornings, that cup of coffee just isn't enough gas to get the motor running. And then there are other mornings we just want to bury our heads in the covers and stay in bed. "Just an extra thirty minutes pleassse," we murmur as the children begin to wake-up.

In our pursuits of portraying this perfect mirror image of a wife and mom; we begin spreading ourselves paper thin. A mom's worst nightmare is becoming so weary that we actually become physically sick. For the stay at home mom, a sick day is just that—a day of being sick while still having to care for the children and home. Can anybody else relate?

In well-doing, we need strength and stamina to endure all hardships. In times of weakness, when our flesh fails us we need a source of strength! My dear stay at home mom, if you think your flesh will not fail you time and time again you are in for a rude awakening. Doing things in our own strength sets us up for failure, frustration, anxiety, stress, and depression. Let's examine ourselves right now; are you leaning on your own strengths and abilities? Or, are you leaning on your ultimate source of divine strength given to you by God?

When we fully submit ourselves to God and his will for our lives; the pressures and burdens of life begin to lighten little-by-little. As we read our Bibles and spend time in the presence of God, our strength is renewed. We get refueled with hope and faith that we can do this! We can continue to bear this cross as stay at home moms; and with excellence. As we build this intimate relationship with our Heavenly Father, the pressures of this world slowly begin to fade away. Life becomes more enjoyable and we begin loving this opportunity to be a stay at home mom!

You Are Strong

The LORD gives strength to his people; the LORD blesses his people with peace.

—**Psalms 29:11**

Strength and honor are her clothing; She shall rejoice in time to come.—**Proverbs 31:25**

The Lord is my strength and my shield;
My heart trusted in Him, and I am helped;
Therefore my heart greatly rejoices,
And with my song I will praise Him.

Psalms 28:7

She girds herself with strength, And strengthens her arms.

—**Proverbs 31:17**

✝

PRAYER & CONFESSION

Dear Heavenly Father, we sing praises unto you because you are so good. Our hearts rejoice because you're our daily source of strength. As we renew our minds in your word, we thank you for a refreshing that strengthens us physically, mentally, as well as spiritually. We declare and decree that we are girded with strength as we complete our daily tasks as stay at home moms.

We pray that in well doing, we will not become weary. We thank you that we are clothed not only in strength but in honor as we manage our children and homes with excellence. Lord Jesus, you are our strength and our shield. Shield us from any stress and negative feelings that may try to consume us. We thank you for your grace and mercy that renews with each morning. In Jesus name we pray. Amen.

You Are Empowered

God is in the midst of her, she shall not be moved; God shall help her, just at the break of dawn.

—**Psalms 46:5**

Blessed is she who believed, for there will be a fulfillment of those things which were told her from the Lord."—**Luke 1:45**

But by the grace of God I am what I am, and His grace toward me was not in vain; but I labored more abundantly than they all, yet not I, but the grace of God which was with me.

1 Corinthians 15:10

I will praise You, for I am fearfully and wonderfully made; Marvelous are Your works, And that my soul knows very well.—**Psalms 139:14**

✝

PRAYER & CONFESSION

Dear Lord, we marvel at your wonderful works. We acknowledge that you have empowered us to be more than conquerors through Christ Jesus. We are fearfully and wonderfully made as "mommagers". By your grace, you make us strong, honorable, and we do not labor in vain. Lord, we give you the glory because you are in our midst. Even when we feel so far from you; you are right here with us stirring up our faith, instilling in us courage, power, and divine strength.

According to Psalms 121, our help comes from the Lord, the creator of heaven and earth. According to 2 Corinthians 12:9, your divine strength is made perfect in our weakness. Glory be to God that we do not have to be weary in our pursuit as stay at home moms. Your grace is sufficient enough for each of us to prevail! We give you the honor and the praise. In Jesus name. Amen.

Conclusion

Woman of God, utilize this tool to combat the negative feelings that afflict our every existence as stay at home moms. Pray these prayers, confess these scriptures, and more importantly allow the Holy spirit to impart the wisdom, knowledge, and understanding of His word in your heart. I pray you come to realize that you are important, perfectly capable, and have the strength to endure the worst of days. Your mandate and mantle as a "mommager" is your first ministry! Learning to combat these negative feelings and extinguishing every fiery dart that Satan throws at us, is key to walking in your full authority as a wife, mother, homemaker, and Woman of Valor!

FHG

FOR HIS GLORY

"Giving Your Ministry A Voice"

https://www.forhisglorywc.com
https://www.facebook.com/forhisglorywc

ABOUT THE AUTHOR

Jasmine Frost is an anointed content strategist, editor, author, and blogger. She is the owner and operator of For His Glory Writing Co. established in 2018. She is also an editor and contributing writer for Miller Media Group; a media company started by Jamal and Natasha Miller of Married & Young.

Jasmine's company, For His Glory Writing Co., has recently published a handbook named *The Kingdom Culture Handbook: Cultivating Heaven on Earth* by Apostle Jonathan McKay. This handbook reached #1 in new releases in the category: Christian Church Growth. God has given her a vision to write content specifically for the Christian niche to inspire, convict, and convert audiences to Christ.

Jasmine Frost has released her first self-published work, a daily devotional named *Strength: A Daily Devotional For The Stay At Home Mom*, available for purchase on Amazon. This daily devotional reached the #1 new release on Amazon in two categories: One-Hour Religion and Spirituality Short Reads. For His Glory Writing Co. has partnered with ministries around the nation to create an online magazine that spotlights the creative abilities of God's people as authors, artists, and ministers of the Gospel. *FHG (For His Glory)*

Magazine will be released January of 2019 and available upon Subscription!

To learn more about Jasmine Frost and her company, For His Glory Writing Co., visit the website and Facebook page:

https://www.forhisglorywc.com
https://www.facebook.com/forhisglorywc/

We Want to Hear From You!

Do You Have a Testimony?

Do You Have a Praise Report?

Did You Enjoy This Read?

Did This Devotional Help You?

Send us an email at:

forhisglorywritingco@gmail.com

Or You can write us at:

For His Glory Writing Co.
5792 Lakeshore Drive
Bean Station, TN 37708

Made in the USA
Lexington, KY
18 November 2019